Gun Control

by

Aaron Powell

This book is a work of fiction. Names, characters, places, and incidents are either products of the author's imagination or are used fictitiously. Any resemblance to actual events or locales or persons, living or dead, is entirely coincidental.

www.aaronbpowell.com

ISBN-13: 978-1484134405

ISBN-10: 1484134400

© Can Stock Photo Inc. / curioustiger

Gun Control

A father and his two young sons are sitting in their living room watching the news. A reporter on CNN is talking about gun control and the possibility of the Supreme Court reviewing the Second Amendment in response to the Sandy Hook Elementary School shooting. The sons, Corbin and Hudson, are curious about all of the recent talk about gun control. Corbin, the older of the two boys, turns to his father in an effort to clarify the meaning of all that has happened.

Corbin: Dad, why do they keep talking about all

of these shootings on the news?

Father: Well, people are very concerned about

all of the violence that's been going on

in our country. The media is trying to

increase awareness and get everyone to

pay attention.

Corbin: But why does the government want to

take away our guns?

Father: There are a lot of people in our country

who think taking away some of the guns will prevent all of this violence and senseless killing.

Hudson: Do you think it will, Daddy?

Father: Not really, son.

Hudson: Why not?

Father: Many people think if the government takes away certain types of guns and some of the accessories, like the magazines we use for our rifles, they will lessen the number of people that are hurt and killed. The idea makes sense, right?

Hudson: Uh-huh.

Father: What do you think, Corbin?

Corbin: Well...won't the people who use the

guns to hurt others still want to do bad things?

Father: That's exactly right, son. Controlling the types of guns and ammunition and keeping guns away from people who want to commit acts of violence probably won't fix anything. Taking things away isn't fixing the people who want to hurt others. Gun control is a way to treat the symptoms. It prevents the extent of violence. Maybe when people want to grab a gun and do something bad, they'll have to think about it for a while, and hopefully they'll cool down and change their minds. But minimizing the extent of violence doesn't really prevent anything. Some people get so mad or depressed that they will find a way to hurt someone because they think lashing out will make things better.

Corbin: But their action would be harder, more personal.

Hudson: Not if they used explosives or poison!

Corbin: Shut up, Hudson.

Father: No, your brother's right, Corbin. People were finding ways to hurt each other long before guns were around. For example, in some countries, citizens carried swords and knives. People are more creative than you might think, especially when they're very motivated.

Corbin: I guess I didn't think about that.

Father: Sometimes when something is so

obvious, we can't see it right in front of

us. Just remember the point we've

made here: the intent is the issue, not

the means. The intent to commit

violence will not necessarily go away if

the means is taken away. Understand?

The boys eagerly nod their heads.

Corbin: So Dad, why do politicians try to take

away the guns and not help the people

not to want to commit violence?

Father: I'm glad you asked me that, son. To

understand politics, we must first

understand the politician. He does not

reflect and consider things objectively

as I have taught you, such as we are doing right now. The politician is pressured by uninformed and ignorant citizens and the people and companies that offer him money to support and voice their opinions. It has nothing to do with what is moral and just.

Hudson: The politicians do what we tell them to do?

Father: That's pretty accurate, but if we aren't thinking rationally, our politicians aren't going to make rational decisions on our behalf.

Corbin: But, Dad, couldn't we just—

Father: *Could* we.

Corbin: *Could* we just get people to help sick

people so they don't want to hurt
others?

Father: That's a good question, son. YES, we
certainly could, and we should.
Unfortunately, even if we were thinking
rationally and asking our politicians—
our congressmen—to do things like
help prevent people from wanting to
commit violence, someone with more
money who wants guns taken away for
some other reason could have more
influence than we do.

Corbin: I don't understand, Dad. Why is our
government so screwed up?

Father: Our government is a reflection of our

people—our businesses and our society. I think fewer and fewer people are paying attention and thinking about why things are the way they are. Think about Communist countries, such as North Korea and China. Their citizens aren't allowed to have guns, and they are easily terrorized and manipulated by their corrupt governments. That's why some people—like me—are concerned about the direction society seems to be going. Americans are willing to give up their freedoms so they don't have to think or worry about anything. This thinking is very dangerous, and all we have to do is sit back and let it happen. We're allowing our Second Amendment to be restructured and diluted, and eventually it could be abolished altogether.

Hudson: Dad, why do we even have a Second Amendment? What is it?

Corbin: Seriously, Hudson?

Father: Now, Corbin, I want you to try and appreciate your little brother's questions. The fact of the matter is that many of the same people who want to get rid of guns don't understand why we were allowed to have them in the first place. Your brother hasn't learned yet, but we are going to teach him.

Sadly, there are too many Americans who can't answer this question, and what's worse is they don't care. All right, Corbin, let's hear the answer.

Corbin: Well, the Second Amendment is the right to own and bear arms, which means guns. It's so average people like us can protect ourselves from criminals and oppression. Like, if our government tries to do something that's bad, like an unlawful order, we can protect ourselves and stop them.

Father: That's pretty good, son. Try not to say 'like' while you're thinking about your answer. Be confident and take your time.

Hudson: Dad, why would our government try to do something bad?

Father: Hopefully, it never will, but think about countries that don't allow private ownership of firearms. Their citizens don't have a Second Amendment, and their governments became corrupt. The citizens of those countries couldn't protect themselves by deterring their tyrannical government.

Corbin: Yeah, but that would never happen here, right Dad?

Father: It's hard to say, Corbin. It seems pretty farfetched, but consider what's happening with North Korea and the way the Bush Administration handled

Iraq and 9/11. America doesn't look so great to the rest of the world lately. Having guns around deters foreign invaders, too.

Hudson: We could be invaded?

Father: If enough of America's enemies joined together and tricked us somehow, they sure could. What if North Korea is backed by China, the Middle East, and our bases in Japan and Africa are overrun? Who can we count on to come to *our* aid? All of a sudden, *we'll* be the guerillas, like the Viet Cong and the insurgents in Iraq and Afghanistan. We can't fight a war with shotguns and pistols.

Corbin: But our military will protect us. You're a Marine, Dad. Other veterans will fight and protect us.

Father: Of course, the veterans will band together. But what if we don't have any guns? And our military will be busy everywhere else except here if our enemies plan an invasion, right?

Hudson: The police?

Father: The police aren't really trained to fight a war. Many of them are veterans, though, and hopefully they would get help from other civilians. The point is that we would be worse off if our enemies knew our government took away our guns. It's a weakness they could capitalize on.

Corbin: Oh, I never really thought that was possible.

Father: It's not always easy to see things from another point of view, especially when we are so used to feeling safe in our own country all the time. Imagine what it would be like to be a Vietnamese or Iraqi boy when the Americans invaded their countries, or how the natives felt when Japan invaded the Philippines. Americans assume that they are safe, but this assumption is just an illusion we have created for ourselves by not paying attention.

Corbin and Hudson sit quietly as they process all that their father has discussed with them. After a few moments have passed, Hudson has another concern.

Hudson: Dad, if people like us know all of this stuff, why do other Americans want to get rid of guns? I hear people say that we should ban *all* guns. Why would they think like that?

Father: Think about it this way, Hudson. You two have gone hunting with your grandpa. I am a former Marine, and I enjoy target shooting with you guys. We know that we're always very careful.

Hudson: And you keep the guns and

ammunition locked up, and we don't

know the combinations.

Father: That's right, buddy, for all of our

protection. Also, so nobody can come

and steal them, but it's easy for a

citizen or a politician who have no use

for guns to dismiss them and side with

anti-gun legislation.

Corbin: Yeah, just like it's easy for a politician to

send another family's son to fight a war

that has no just cause while they keep

their own kids out of the war. It's not

fair.

Father: OK, Corbin. Nice analogy. It's good to

see you thinking for yourself, but let's

stay focused on gun control.

Hudson: I feel bad for the moms and dads who lost their kids to violence.

Father: I'm glad you do, Hudson. I don't know what I would do if anything like that ever happened to you boys. My heart would break.

Corbin: You would get revenge, wouldn't you, Dad?

Father: I would be very angry, but I don't think that would fix anything. Retaliation is a powerful human urge. Our emotions can get the best of us; that's why people commit acts of violence in the first place. But it's not a logical reaction, and I think most of the families have to come to terms with what has happened to them and we should do what we can

to support them.

Corbin: Yeah, I guess that makes sense. I would

be pretty crazy if my kid was murdered.

Father: Of course, you would. I'm pleased that

my boys are so concerned with

something so tragic. I hope that you will

always be respectful toward the victims

and their families. It's interesting that

many of these families are less

concerned with gun control and are

more focused on addressing and

correcting what drives people to turn to

violence.

Hudson: We will, Dad.

Father: I know you will. I love you boys very

much. It's important to your mom and me that you boys not only respect the opinions of others, but that you are also confident and stand up for your own opinions. If you're ever feeling down or something happens that makes you really mad, don't be afraid or ashamed to talk about it with your mom and me or even with each other or a good friend. Sometimes life can be very hard, and you can feel very alone, but it's up to you to ask for help so we can change something to make life better. No one should ever feel so cornered that they turn to violence. Do you understand me?

Hudson: Yes, Dad.

Corbin: Yes, Dad.

Father: Good. I'm proud of you boys. Now get

your butts upstairs and brush your

teeth.

GUNS ARE NOT THE ISSUE: WE ARE.

About the Author

Aaron Powell served as a marine during Operation Iraqi Freedom and Operation Enduring Freedom. He graduated from the University of North Carolina at Wilmington in 2003 with a BA in criminal justice and a psychology minor. He also completed a second BA in business administration at Ashford University, where he graduated with distinction in 2011. Aaron Powell is a prolific writer, an avid reader, and is an active marksman. Aaron and his wife and sons live near Austin, Texas.

www.ingramcontent.com/pod-product-compliance
Lightning Source LLC
Chambersburg PA
CBHW071344310526
45790CB00018B/1351